THE
SALES
COACH

THE
SALES
COACH

MICHAEL PATTERSON

The Sales Coach

Published by:
Tremendous Life Books
118 West Allen Street
Mechanicsburg, PA 17055

717-766-9499   800-233-2665
Fax: 717-766-6565

www.TremendousLifeBooks.com

ISBN: 978-1-936354-45-0

DEDICATION

For Kyleigh,
The world is your stage;
give your best performance.

TABLE OF CONTENTS

INTRODUCTION

If you are reading this book, there's a good chance your job involves selling. In my 25 year career I've worked for a number of financial institutions, ranging from a small community credit union to one of the nation's largest commercial banks, and I've held positions that have encompassed all aspects of the sales process, from selling directly to customers to managing, recruiting, and training others to sell. If there's anything I've learned it's that selling is an integral part of everyone's job.

EVERYBODY SELLS

If you think you have never sold before, think again: you sold yourself! Remember the interview you went to when you got your job? You were selling yourself to the recruiter or manager. You talked about your skills and explained how those skills provided a benefit to the organization. That's selling. I bet you even started selling as a child, selling your parents on why you should stay up past your bedtime, eat an extra helping of dessert, or get a special toy for your birthday.

SELL IS NOT A FOUR-LETTER WORD

At first glance, some people think *sell* is a four-letter word, but it's really not. There are only three letters in the word; the "L" is repeated. This is a good analogy for why some employees are hesitant to sell; just as *sell* isn't really a four-letter word, the act of selling may not be exactly what they think it is. Many think that selling is being pushy and forcing unnecessary products on customers when real, needs-based selling is not about that at all. It's about offering solutions to solve a customer's problems. Customers purchase products to fill a need or a want and they are often unsure of what product they need. A salesperson helps guide them to finding a solution.

IT'S ABOUT HAVING CLEAR POOL WATER

I have a swimming pool in my back yard. Each year, around mid-May, I open it up in anticipation of Memorial Day weekend. The first year after we moved into the house, the water looked a little murky, and it didn't clear up right away. I went to the local pool store and explained my situation to the guy behind the counter who diagnosed my problem, suggested a product, and told me how to apply it. The product worked and the pool was ready to use in a few days. Honestly, I went to the store without knowing the problem, only the symptom. My goal wasn't to purchase chemicals; I just wanted to have clear pool water. The salesman sold me a product, but from my point of view he provided a solution. That's needs-based selling.

The story of *The Sales Coach* is one that plays out in real life not only in banks and credit unions, but in every type of business, every single day of the year. I've met a lot of Sallys over the years. Perhaps you've known, managed, or trained a Sally in your day. Maybe you were, or still are, one yourself. As you read the story of *The Sales Coach*, keep your mind open to the sales process. Take some notes to refer back to later. Learn how the best sales plan is about helping the customer attain their needs and wants. I wish you well!

CHAPTER ONE

A NEW SALES CULTURE

Mr. Tom Fox was the new CEO of Friendly Community Bank. Today, all of the employees were gathered for a big company-wide meeting at a large banquet room in the middle of town. The room was decorated with balloons and streamers, upbeat music played over the sound system, and a PowerPoint presentation displayed a mixture of inspiring photos and sayings. Mr. Fox, microphone in hand, strode to the platform.

"Good afternoon, everyone! Today, there is a new focus at Friendly Community Bank. We must change the way we currently do business. Rather than be simply a transactional bank, we will become more focused on serving our customers' needs through sales. Consider it to be a change to a more *sales-centric* culture. Each of you will be responsible for actively talking with our customers, listening to their concerns, discussing product features and benefits, and initiating needs-based selling. We can no longer rely on merely taking orders. We need to *ask* for the business."

"We have a great organization here. Our products and services have the most attractive rates and fees. Our employees are second to none; caring, compassionate, and knowledgeable. Yet my reports show that our typical customer banks with at least three other financial institutions. He or she has more money deposited and borrowed at other banks than he or she does with us. We need to focus more on sales to remain successful."

Sally, a long-time customer service representative, sat along with her colleagues. She listened, but she didn't like what she heard. She felt numb. Sally had always enjoyed working at the bank. She valued her position, and appreciated how much the bank cared about its customers. Now she wasn't so sure. She had heard about how other banks became more focused on getting the sale and less focused on doing what was best for the customer. Some of her co-workers had come from those institutions with horror stories about how they had to pull out all the stops to get more sales. Sure, Mr. Fox had talked about *needs-based* selling, but he also seemed to put down what he referred to as order-takers. That seemed confusing. After all, don't our customers know what they need when they come through the doors?

Sally looked around the room and could tell that others had similar concerns. She heard their grumbling and knew they weren't happy about becoming more 'sales-centric.' She knew her customers wouldn't like the change either. After all, this is a small town with small-town values. Her customers know what they want, and they don't want to be sold products just to meet some quota.

Morale will really go down fast, she thought. Tomorrow is going to be a miserable day at work. Everyone will go home tonight and update their resumes. Maybe she would do the same. She invested so much of her career working at this bank; the thought of starting somewhere new was awful. Everyone at her branch was fearful of the change when Mr. Fox came on board and now all of their fears were coming true.

Sally regained her focus just as the new CEO finished his address.

"I know this change may seem difficult to you at first," Mr. Fox concluded, "but I assure you it will be much easier than it seems. I know you all have what it takes to take Friendly Community Bank to the next level! To assist you in transitioning to this new sales culture, each branch will be provided with its own sales coach to help guide you towards success."

Sally shriveled at his words as she thought about what the future may hold...

CHAPTER TWO

MEETING THE SALES COACH

As Sally predicted, morale took a hit. Like many other employees, she was concerned about how the change was going to impact her, her colleagues, and their customers. The new way of business seemed to replace focusing on service with focusing on sales. Sally wasn't sure if she was cut out for the new culture. After all, she never considered herself a salesperson, never wanted a job where she had to sell, and thought of no good reason why she would want to start now.

When she came to work that day she noticed a man she had never seen before sitting in her manager's office. Maybe that's our sales coach, she thought. Just thinking about having someone train her on how to sell to her customers made Sally feel uneasy. They really were *her* customers, and many of them have been coming in for years. They would often share stories like she was part of their family; stories about their children, a new job, vacations, home remodeling, and dreams about retirement. These people trusted and respected Sally; how could she ever sell them products and services they didn't want?

The man came out of the manager's office and walked toward Sally's desk. He appeared to be in his late thirties, trim, with dark hair. Even though he wore a dark-gray business suit with a crisp light-blue shirt and tie, he appeared very relaxed and friendly. As he approached he smiled and extended his hand. "Hi, you must be Sally. I've heard so much about you from your manager. My name is Dave Kimba, and I'll be your new sales coach." Dave and Sally shook hands. She could tell right away he had an exciting and energetic personality, and radiated a vibe that made her feel that even though they had just met, they were old friends.

"Hello, Mr. Kimba, it's nice to meet you" replied Sally.

"Please call me Dave. Anytime someone says Mr. Kimba I automatically look around to see if my dad is behind me! It really is great to meet you. I'm very excited we have an opportunity to work together."

Sally began the day skeptical of the sales culture, and by association, skeptical of her sales coach as well. But Dave made a great first impression, and he was someone who was tough not to like. He definitely didn't come across like an uptight banker, nor did he look the part of a smarmy salesman, the type you envision walking the lot of a used-car dealership. He had piqued her interest, and Sally was at least mildly curious about what the new sales coach was going to say.

"Sally, I was doing some research about the bank, its customers, and employees before I came here today" Dave informed her. "I know about the long, proud history of Friendly Community Bank and how it's served your customers for almost a hundred years. I also know how much you value your relationship with your customers. Customers feel comfortable and welcome in the branches. They like to share stories and show pictures. And now the culture is changing; employees were never expected to sell before and many are leery of the change."

Sally was impressed. Dave had done his homework.

"Most of all," Dave continued, "I learned a lot about you. I know you've been here for a long time. I know how much you embody the spirit of the company. You take great pride in the quality of work you perform here. And I especially know how much you care about your customers. You've been recognized by the company for your high level of customer service. You treat customers as if they were your own brother or sister. That is why I'm really excited to be working with you. I think out of everyone in the company, you are going to be the most successful in this new sales climate."

Sally was flattered by everything Dave was said about her. As a matter of fact, she got a little embarrassed. She did take pride in her work, and she did care about her customers like they were her own brothers and sisters. However, the last comment was where Dave was wrong. Sally didn't consider herself to be a salesperson, and didn't know how she would muster up the courage to ask for a single sale, not to mention being the most successful salesperson in the bank. Sally told Dave about her trepidation. She stressed to him that for as long as she had been there, the bank was all about providing quality customer service. She was unhappy about the change to a sales culture, and didn't think her customers would appreciate the new culture either. After all, they are hard-working, blue-collar people who can't afford to pay for extra products and services they don't need.

Dave listened intently and responded sympathetically. "Sally, I completely understand how you feel. I am truly inspired by your commitment to providing service to your customers, which again is exactly why I believe you will be the most successful salesperson in the entire organization."

Sally seemed confused and asked Dave to tell her more.

"I'm going to let you in on a secret. It's my number-one rule of sales. It's so important that I'm going to write it down for you."

Dave took out a small notebook from the inside pocket of his jacket and jotted down three words in big letters for Sally to see:

SALES IS SERVICE!

Sally was puzzled. She had always thought of sales and service as two opposite things.

"Think about it; when customers come into the branch with a question about their transactions or account balances, they come and see you. Customers rely on you to help with a financial need or concern. You provide them solutions to their problems, and those solutions are in the form of products and services."

Dave continued, "The most successful salespeople are those who cultivate relationships with their customers. I'm not only talking about banking; it's true for all types of business. Sally, from what I've heard, you've cultivated deeper and more meaningful relationships with your customers than anyone else in the entire organization. That's why I keep saying that you are going to have great success with the new culture here. Some people hear the word sales and immediately have a negative image in their head. They think sales is a bad thing, probably because they've been on the receiving end of people doing sales the wrong way. They've experienced employees selling for the sole purpose of reaching goals and getting to the bottom line. Real selling is just the opposite of that. Successful sales are all about providing service. Robert Kiyosaki said it best in his book, *Rich Dad, Poor Dad*: 'True selling is caring, listening, solving problems, and serving your fellow human being.'

"Listen, it's my job to be your sales coach. Beginning next Monday, we'll meet every day for the entire week. Over that time we are going to work together to learn all about needs-based selling and how to sell through service. I want to show you how trust and ethics play a big part in sales. We'll talk about how to uncover your customers' financial needs and match them with a product or service to better serve them. We'll determine why customers perform certain transactions and learn how they lead to sales opportunities. Let me make a deal with you: I will never ask you to sell a product or service just to meet a quota. I will never expect you to make a sale unless it completely benefits the customer. But I do expect when you discover that opportunity, you do ask for the sale.

"Before we start next week, there's something I need you to do. Have you ever gone into a store to talk about a product and had the impression the salesperson didn't know much more than you did?"

"Yes" replied Sally. "A few months ago I bought a new camera for my husband's birthday. He's starting to take up photography as a hobby, and wanted something better than his cell phone or basic-model camera. I wanted to buy him one of those digital cameras that you can add a special zoom lens and external flash to. When I got to the electronic store to ask the salesperson questions about it, he didn't do much more than read the information off of the card by the display. I could have done that! He even gave me wrong information. He told me the camera would take the same memory card as our old camera but it didn't. I had to go back later to buy a different card. What a terrible experience!"

"I agree that was a terrible experience, Sally" agreed Dave. "The salesperson, and I use that term loosely, broke my number-two rule of sales:

You Can't Sell What You Don't Know

"As a salesperson, your job is to educate your customers about how your products and services benefit them. If you don't know how a product works or how it makes someone's life easier or more enjoyable, you can't sell it. A salesperson needs to educate the customer on every aspect of the products for sale. There are a lot of different accounts, loans, and other products and services offered here at the bank. Before we begin to meet next week I need you to know them inside and out. I'm not talking about general product knowledge,

I'm talking about understanding everything you offer; balances, fees, rates, and so on. You need to know which products and services complement each other. You also need to know your target audience, what type of customer would be the best."

Sally nodded in agreement to everything Dave said. She was pretty confident she knew her products, but now she was going to review them again just to make extra sure. The last thing she wanted to do was to let down her customers by not having an answer if they asked about how a service works, or even worse, give them wrong information.

"I'm looking forward to beginning on Monday, Sally" said Dave as he shook her hand and left. Although still a little skeptical, Sally was looking forward to Monday as well.

Sally's Notebook

☑ Sales is Service.

☑ You can't sell what you don't know.

☑ The most successful salespeople are those who cultivate relationships with their customers.

☑ The salesperson's job is to educate customers about how their products and services benefit them.

CHAPTER THREE

THE CUSTOMER COMPASS

Monday morning, the first day Sally was to start working with her new sales coach, she came into the branch to find a small toy compass on her desk. Accompanying the compass was a handwritten note:

> Before you know which direction
> to take your customers, you
> need to know where they come
> from and how they got here.
>   Dave

Sally picked up the compass and studied it for a short while before reading the note again. I wonder what it means, she thought. More specifically, she wondered how it related to sales. She knew she didn't need to wait too long, as Dave was scheduled to meet with her within the hour. Skeptical at first, now she was anxious to get her sales coaching started.

"Good morning, Sally," greeted Dave, "I think today is going to be a great day. Did you get the present I left for you?"

"I did" said Sally as she held out the small compass. "I've been curious about what it meant from the moment I read your note. Luckily we were meeting this morning. I don't know if I could have waited all day!"

"Today we begin to understand your customers," Dave explained. "Understanding your customers is the key to sales. Do you know the biggest mistakes salespeople make?"

Sally shook her head.

"The biggest mistake is that they treat all customers like their needs are the same. We know that everyone is different in their own way, and we need to understand how our customers have different interests, goals, and expectations. What is important to one person may not be important to another. There are different reasons that drive customers to do business with any company, and a bank is no different. Not only do we treat customers like their needs are the same, we subconsciously do something even worse; we treat them like their needs are the same as *our* needs. This brings us to my third rule of sales:

Focus on What's Important to the Customer, Not What's Important to You

"I once received a phone call from an insurance company trying to get me to switch homeowner's coverage. Their entire sales pitch focused on how much cheaper their premiums were compared to what I was currently paying. The person on the other end of the phone thought the most important thing to me was saving money. Now I'm sure a lot of people would be interested in saving as much money as they could on insurance, and I like to save money as much as the next person. But a few years ago there was a really bad storm which knocked down a lot of trees in the area. One fell on my roof and another on my neighbor's across the street. When I called my insurance agent, she was really helpful. The tree was cut down, the roof repaired, and the check received in no time. It took my neighbor almost three times as long to get his situation rectified after countless calls to his insurance company. I know I may pay a little more for my insurance, but the peace of mind is worth it. When a salesperson is more focused on his or her needs instead of the customer's, a sales opportunity is lost before it even begins. That's why we need to focus less on what's important to us and more on what's important to our customers. That's where the compass comes in. You need to understand what direction the customer is coming from and how they got there to determine which direction they need to go."

Dave asked Sally to take out a blank piece of paper, draw a compass, and label the four points **N**, **S**, **E**, and **W**.

"Did you ever notice the points of the compass spell out the word *news?*" asked Dave.

"What is the news, but a way to present information? The information you learn from the news can help you prepare for your days ahead and to make better decisions. If you hear that it's going to rain tomorrow afternoon, you know to bring an umbrella to work. If you hear it's going to be sunny and pleasant, you plan to take a walk in the park or let your kids outside to play. If you hear there is an accident on the freeway, you plan on taking a different route to work. So let's look at what type of information the NEWS provides us about our customers, and learn how it will make us more successful salespeople. The letter **N** stands for **Needs**. These are bear-minimum, non-negotiable. Your customers can't function without them. Needs are almost never products; they are issues or concerns which are addressed by certain products. A customer has bills, and needs a way to pay them. A checking account provides a solution to that need.

An individual has a cold and needs to get better, so he or she goes to a pharmacy to buy cold medicine."

"The letter **W** stands for **Wants**. These are the customer's goals, aspirations, and dreams. A customer wants a new pool in the backyard or to take a cruise. Wants are different from needs; be careful not to confuse the two. While both are important, they are quite different. I need transportation to get to work or to go other places. There isn't any public transportation I can rely on, so I need a car. But I don't need a brand-new car, and definitely don't need a luxury car. That type of car is a want, not a need."

"Some businesses sell more needs than wants. Banks are typically a business that sells needs-based products and services. Most people don't *want* a checking accounting; they need it. I'm not going to invite my friends over to look at my new checking account like I would a big-screen TV. Customers need a way to pay their bills; therefore, they need a checking account. Customers also need our accounts to help secure their wants. A customer who wants a new car may need a car loan to pay for it. Another customer who wants to retire at 55 needs an investment account and budgetary services to afford to do so. Other businesses sell needs-based products as well, such as a pharmacies and gas stations."

"Some businesses sell mainly want-based products and services. These businesses deal with discretionary-spending items such as jewelry, artwork, vacations, and entertainment. Some businesses offer a combination of both. The grocery store is a great example of this. Everyone needs food to survive, and the grocery store sells food. But it also sells want-based foods such as snacks, desserts, and ready-made meals. Have you ever seen employees offering free samples at the grocery store? They are almost always for want types of products. That's why they say you should never go grocery shopping when you're hungry, Sally!"

Sally took frantic notes as Dave described the difference between needs and wants. She had never really thought about it until today's conversation.

"The **E** stands for **Emotions**. Customers make buying decisions based on emotions all the time, some bad and some good. I've always heard you should never go shopping when you are upset, and you should never go to the food store when you're hungry. In both instances, emotions cloud your judgment and you end up spending more than you wanted or needed to spend. Emotions can also prevent a sale from happening. When people make a big purchase, oftentimes they are worried about spending too much money. The same is true in banking when customers are concerned with investing money or taking out a loan."

The **S** stands for **Sacrifices**. What is it your customers are willing to sacrifice in order to attain their needs and wants? Investing is all about sacrifice. Some people will s*acrifice* income because they *need* the safety of an insured savings account. Other people are willing to *sacrifice* security because they *want* high returns. Outside of banking, many people are willing to pay for convenience. Tell me, Sally, if you needed to pick up a gallon of milk, would you be more likely to stop at a convenience store on the way home, knowing you are going to pay an extra dollar or so, or would you save the money and go to the big grocery store further down the road?"

"I would pay the extra money at the convenience store," rationalized Sally, "because it's much more convenient than parking my car, walking through the grocery store, and waiting in line"

"Exactly," said Dave. "In this case you are willing to sacrifice money for convenience. But maybe someone else couldn't afford the extra money and thought it was better to go to the grocery store. That person is willing to sacrifice their time to save money. Or maybe next time, you have some free time to kill. The point is, people are willing to make some sacrifices for wants and needs, but those sacrifices change from person to person, and may even change for the same person depending on the situation."Remember a few minutes ago when I talked about the traffic report on the news?"

"I do," said Sally.

"The people in those cars all came from different starting points and they all end up someplace different. They traveled in different cars and took different routes. But they all have a destination in mind, a goal. Sales are like that, Sally. It's our job to assist customers on their journey to reach their goal. We don't know where they're going and we don't know where they came from unless we find out. That's why we need to learn the member compass. I can't give everyone on the road the same directions, because it's not going to take everyone where they want to be. That's why I said earlier that salespeople often make a big mistake by assuming customers share the same needs and wants. They end up trying to sell the same products and services to the same customers. They don't know to understand what brought the customers in and where they're going. Have you ever gone into that big sporting goods store in the mall?"

"Yes, I have," replied Sally. "My son plays baseball for his high school. We go to that store a lot."

"Have you ever noticed how each time you go in, they always tell you that socks are on sale, two packs for $10?"

"Yes!" said Sally. "Every time I purchase something, or if we're just looking around in the aisles, someone is trying to sell us socks. Socks may make sense if we're buying new sneakers, but why would I be interested in socks if we're buying a new baseball glove?"

"Exactly," replied Dave. "The salespeople there are taking part in what we call *pushing product*. No matter what you come in for, they're going to talk to you about socks. It doesn't take a really astute customer to realize he or she is being 'sold', and that will start to turn off the customers to *other* sales. You see, Sally, customers don't mind that you are *selling*, they just don't want to be *sold*."

Sally nodded her head in agreement. "This is the main reason why I was always hesitant to sell," she said. "I never wanted to force anything on customers that they didn't want or need. I guess that's why it's important to learn the customer compass so you can understand their needs and wants, along with their emotions and sacrifices."

"Now you're starting to get it!" exclaimed Dave. "Everybody is a good fit for some product, and every product is a good fit for somebody, but every product isn't a fit for everybody. When you make the right connection based on the customer compass, sales starts to be easy. This is only the beginning, Sally. Tomorrow we'll learn more."

Sally couldn't wait. With a coach like Dave, maybe she could learn to like the new sales culture.

Sally's Notebook

☑ Focus on what's important to the customer, not what's important to you.

☑ Understand the NEWS about the customer: Needs, Emotions, Wants, and Sacrifices.

☑ Customers don't mind that you're selling, but they don't want to be sold.

CHAPTER FOUR

SOMEONE TO LIKE AND TRUST

On Tuesday morning, Sally again found a note, this time with just three words written on it:

Ethos

Pathos

Logos

For the second day in a row, Sally was curious. She wondered what those words meant. Her curiosity would have to hold on a little longer today than yesterday though, because she was not scheduled to meet with Dave until after lunch. The morning was a little slow, and customer interaction sporadic. When she did have a customer, she expanded on her conversations more than she would have in the past, discovering their needs, wants, emotions, and sacrifices just like she had learned the day before. Sally always found customers easy to talk with, and came to realize their NEWS was always right in front of her, she just never knew to pay attention before yesterday.

Just after noon, Dave came into the branch. They exchanged greetings and Sally briefly told him about the customer interactions she had that morning, and how easy it was to discuss needs and wants with them. Before long, the conversation turned to the note left near Sally's desk. She was curious to find out about ethos, pathos, and logos.

"I knew it would pique your interest. Have you ever heard them before?" asked Dave.

"I really don't know," confessed Sally. "At first I thought they were the names of the Three Musketeers."

Dave let out a laugh before he caught himself. "I apologize for laughing. That's a good guess, though. Ethos, pathos, and logos are not the Three Musketeers, but they do embody the spirit of 'all for one and one for all.' They are the three components that make up a great sales presentation to your customer. All three of them are needed to be successful.

"I took a philosophy class in college, and was enamored with all the great Greek philosophers. Aristotle was a famous Greek philosopher who studied under Plato and was credited with teaching Alexander the Great how to give a proper speech, articulate his thoughts, and get his audience to understand his points. In about 300 B.C. Aristotle wrote a book *The Art of Rhetoric*. In it he identified the three key methods of persuasion: Ethos, Pathos, and Logos. A great salesperson must be able to deliver a great presentation to his or her customers about the company's products and services. To do that, you must possess those three qualities."

Ethos is the Greek word for character or ethics. It represents your credibility. Without credibility, you cannot truly develop a relationship with your customer. Sally, your customers need to trust you to be an honest, ethical person who is concerned about his or her financial well-being. Last week we talked about the importance of knowing your products and services inside and out. Yesterday we discussed determining customers' needs and wants and understanding how those needs and wants differ from customer to customer. Ethos pulls all of that together. It requires you to be an expert in your company's products and services, with distinct knowledge about how each will meet the needs and the wants of each particular customer. Ethos is communicated through everything you say and do; your words, tone, style, dress, workstation appearance, and other conduct."

Sally listened intently as Dave talked about the importance of ethos. She thought of the many times she had been a customer herself, dealing with a salesperson who didn't seem concerned about her as a person, or didn't really know their products. She acknowledged how hesitant she was to make a purchase from those salespeople.

"*Pathos* is the Greek word for experience," continued Dave. "It refers to the emotional and imaginative impact of your message. Yesterday we learned about the customer compass, and how every member has needs and wants and sacrifices they are willing to give up to attain those needs and wants. We also talked about customer emotion, and how those emotions sometimes help and can also hinder customers. We talked about how emotions can either drive some people to a sale or away from one. We also talked about how everyone has a different compass, and customers all have different places where they started and places they want to go. Sally, a great salesperson must truly listen to the customer and be able to understand their compass. And when you do, pathos means you need to communicate it to them by using empathy and effective storytelling to which the customer can relate."

"I remember last Christmas I was in a store buying a toy for one of my children. There was a display of batteries near the register. The cashier asked me if I wanted to purchase any, but I didn't think I needed any and declined. A couple weeks later I came back into the same store for another toy. This time when I was checking out, a different cashier was at the register. She told me it looked like I was buying a fun toy, asked me if I was buying it as a gift, and if I had children. She then shared with me a short story:

> *'I love Christmas mornings. It's always a lot of fun watching the kids tearing into their gifts and so excited to play with their new toys. They tend to get a lot of electronic toys. Sometimes my husband can't remember if we have batteries or not. Fortunately, I always stock up on them when they're on sale. They're on sale today if you happen to need any.'"*

"Not surprisingly, I ended up purchasing the pack of batteries. The cashier presented a story to which I could relate, and grabbed at my emotions. I've been in the situation before when we needed batteries but didn't have any and I sure wouldn't want to be in that predicament on Christmas morning. I thought spending a few dollars was well worth the peace of mind."

"The final piece is *logos*, or logic. It refers to the ability to appeal to an individual's intellect. Sales are about providing a solution to a customer's needs and wants, but the solution needs to make sense to them. This can be done by providing concrete facts and figures to support your recommendation."

"To be effective, all three qualities must work hand in hand with each other. Just like the Three Musketeers: all for one and one for all. Let's say you're talking to a customer about how he or she can save money by refinancing their loan with your bank. Ethos gives you the credibility to present the option to your customer and make him or her want to listen to what you have to offer. Pathos is how you convey it to the customer to align with their compass. In this case you key in on a major want—saving money. Logos is presenting the facts such as rate and monthly payment amount to back up your claim. If you can't back up your claim, you begin to lose credibility for the next time you talk with a customer. Can you see how they all tie together?"

"Yes," replied Sally. "I never really gave much thought to it before, but it makes perfect sense. There have been times I've had an uneasy feeling about certain salespeople. To be honest, I felt as if I just couldn't trust them or believe they had my best interests in mind. I felt they looked at me as a dollar sign, not as an individual who came into their store with needs and wants. The same goes for salespeople who didn't seem to try to understand what I needed. They offered me something which just didn't make sense. It seemed more like I was being offered a product of the month rather than something which was suited for me and my situation. I would much rather deal with a person I can trust."

"That's the point exactly!" said Dave. "There's a great book on sales called *Go-Givers Sell More.* In it, the author Bob Burg says, 'All things being equal, people will do more business with, and refer business to, those people they know, like, and trust.' That's such a profound statement I incorporated it into my fourth rule of sales:

BE SOMEONE THE CUSTOMER LIKES AND TRUSTS

"Sally, think about a business you patronize as a consumer. Are you more willing to provide repeat business for someone you trust? Are you more willing to try a new product if someone you trusted recommended it to you, even if there was an added cost involved?"

"Sure I am," replied Sally. "Right away I think about my hairdresser. I've been going to Lorie every six weeks for over ten years. If I forget to make an appointment, I wait for her—even if other stylists are available. I trust her to cut my hair and won't go anywhere else. A year or so ago a competitor opened shop even closer to my house with cheaper prices, but I wouldn't think of going anywhere else. I trust Lorie to cut my hair. Many times she'll recommend a special conditioner or hair gel, and I always purchase it. We have a strong bond and I trust she has my best interest in mind when she makes recommendations. I don't feel treated like a dollar sign."

"That's what the whole concept of sales through service is all about" said Dave. "Most customers are not opposed to an employee 'selling' a product or service. They understand selling is an important aspect of life, and everyone sells. If you aren't selling a product, you're selling an idea, concept, or opinion. While most of us are not opposed to selling, we don't want to be 'sold.' Being 'sold' produces a negative connotation; a belief the employee cares more about selling a product than he does about helping the customer obtain his or her needs and wants. You know Lorie is selling you hair products, and you're OK with it because there's a bond there and a trust that it's truly in your best interest to purchase the product. I knew the cashier at the toy store was selling me batteries, but I really felt she was doing me a favor by doing so."

"One of the keys to building trust and rapport is to create an approachable environment. Employees should be dressed professionally; clothes should be neat, clean, pressed, matching, and worn appropriately. Your workstation should also be neat and free of excess clutter. Employees should possess a friendly and inviting demeanor, approach the customer, and greet him or her. Start by asking for the customer's name and use it. We all like to hear our own name, don't we Sally? Using a customer's name while you initiate non-business conversation helps to put the customer at ease and begins to develop a rapport. Maintain eye contact, which helps develop trust, and smile."

"John Maxwell wrote one of the best books on business: *The 21 Irrefutable Laws of Leadership*. When referring to people's relationships with each other, especially in sales, he said it best:

'People don't care how much you know, until they know how much you care.'"

Sally took notes on everything Dave said, and put her pen down when she heard the last quote. She made a career out of building her reputation and cultivating relationships with her customers, just like her hairdresser, Lorie, had done with her. Sally had always considered sales to be *forcing* products on customers, and now Dave made her realize it was more about building and cultivating relationships. In that very moment it occurred to her she had been preparing to sell for years.

"I think we made a lot of progress these last two days," said Dave, and Sally agreed. "See you tomorrow."

Sally's Notebook

☑ Good sales involves ethos, pathos, and logos; ethics, storytelling, and logic.

☑ Be someone the customer likes and trusts.

☑ Create an approachable environment.

CHAPTER FIVE

UNCOVERING THE NEED

Wednesday was an unexpectedly busy day in the branch. Sally wasn't scheduled to start until 10:30, and by the time she got in there was a line of customers waiting for assistance.

"Hi Sally, I know you're busy" said Mrs. Little, a customer Sally had known for years, "But I just wanted to give you our change of address form. Mr. Little and I are finally settled into our new home. I'm glad we had that yard sale before we moved because there isn't nearly as much room as there was in our old house. But we had all that wasted space once the last of the kids moved out."

Sally took the form from Mrs. Little, wished her well on the new home, and said she would have an opportunity to talk with both Mrs. Little and her husband more the next time they came in. After leaving Mrs. Little, Sally approached the next customer waiting. Sally extended her hand and introduced herself.

"Nice to meet you Sally, my name is Frank." As Sally walked him back to her desk, they engaged in some small talk, discussing how cold it's been outside lately. After exchanging a few more pleasantries, Sally asked him how she could help.

"I came in to get information about your CD rates," replied Frank.

"I can surely get those for you," responded Sally. "I can even print a copy for you to take. This is a great time to invest. You'll find our CD rates are very competitive. You can earn much more money investing in a CD than by leaving your money in a savings account, and CDs are secured by the FDIC, so you won't risk losing any money."

As she was talking, Sally started typing away at her computer to access the current CD rates. Within a few seconds, the rates appeared on her screen, she printed them as promised, handed them to Frank, and asked if there was anything else he needed.

"No," replied Frank. "This is what I was looking for, thank you very much."

"It was my pleasure," said Sally. "I'll be sure to see you when you are ready to deposit." With that, Frank shook Sally's hand and walked out the door. Unbeknownst to Sally, Dave had been in the branch and saw her interaction with both Mrs. Little and Frank.

"Hello, Dave," Sally smiled, "you just missed my first customer of the day. I remembered your lesson from yesterday, and followed the steps we discussed."

"Sally, actually I was here the entire time. It was so crowded, you didn't even see me," said Dave. "I thought I observed you with two customers already, not just one."

"Oh yes, that was Mrs. Little. She's a long-time customer. I wasn't counting that because all she wanted to do was hand me a change of address form."

"OK, we'll talk about that a little later." replied Dave. "First, let's review your interaction with Frank. You did a really good job with everything we talked about yesterday. You demonstrated ethos by the way you conducted yourself and how you started to build a rapport with a good introduction and a personal discussion before talking business. You demonstrated pathos by telling him how profitable and safe investing with the bank would be for him. Finally, you demonstrated logos by printing and showing him the rates and calculations. Remember, Sally, sales is a process. You need to build upon everything we have discussed in order to be successful. Remember Monday when we talked about the customer compass and understanding their needs and wants?"

Sally nodded. "Yes. He wanted to know CD rates."

"That's true on the surface" replied Dave. "But there's more to it than that. You need to dig deeper to uncover the need. Customers' needs can be classified into three categories: *immediate need, future need,* and *unknown need.*

An **immediate need** requires action immediately. This occurs when a customer comes in and wants to do something right away like open an account or apply for a loan. This also happens when a customer has a complaint or a problem, like when someone bounces a check.

A **future need** involves gathering information now, in anticipation of taking action later. This occurs when a customer is expecting money to become available within the next few days, weeks, or months, or when a customer is starting to think about buying a new car.

Frank did come in with what appeared to be an immediate need; he needed CD rates. But he really had a future need: more than likely, he had money to invest in the near future. Sally, as salespeople, we sometimes can't see the actual need on the surface; we have to dig deeper to uncover the actual need. Customers' needs and wants are like an iceberg—we only see the tip of it. The really big part is hidden under water. Unless we dive down, we don't see the whole picture."

Sally understood what Dave was saying. "It makes sense Frank didn't just want to know the rates for the sake of knowing the rates. He wanted to know because he was going to invest money. I guess it's like going to look at dresses when you know you have a wedding or big event coming up. You're not ready to buy right then, you're just trying to determine styles and prices to prepare for when it's time to buy; a future need, it makes sense. Tell me Dave, how do I handle that in the future? Is there something I should have asked?"

"Absolutely," responded Dave. "Whenever a customer comes to gather information, you're dealing with a future need. In those situations there are a few questions you want to ask. These questions work for all sales, not just banking. I call them the three hows: *how much, how soon,* and *how will* you use.

- **How much** tells you how much they plan to spend, borrow, or invest.

- **How soon** tells you when they plan to take action.

- **How will** you use helps determine the best product or service to fit their need.

When Frank came in today to ask about CD rates, asking him how much he planned to invest helped determine the best product to offer him. I read that the bank has a $1,000 minimum deposit for CDs. Suppose Frank didn't know that and only had $500 to invest. When he came back into the branch, he may have felt embarrassed to discover that he didn't have enough. That surely wouldn't help you in attaining ethos."

"Asking the customer how much makes perfect sense," said Sally. "Also, we have a higher rate if the customer is depositing more than $75,000. But I don't understand asking how they plan to use it. If the customer wants to deposit money, obviously they are going to spend it at some point."

"You're right," replied Dave, "but the how and why make a big difference. In banking, customers have short-term and long-term goals. Let's say Frank was saving to buy a home or to pay for a wedding in the next few years. That limits the amount of time he could reasonably invest. Let's say he was saving for retirement. In that case he may have ten years or more to invest. Now he may be interested in investing in longer terms or even other products such as stocks or mutual funds."

"A lot of customers don't even know we have an employee who is licensed to sell those products. If I didn't at least tell Frank about the option of investing in them he may have gone to another bank down the street and invested with them instead. I was always worried about giving the customer too many choices. But I guess the *how soon* question lets me know when Frank wants to invest his money, and tells me if he has time to review the information and meet with our investment consultant."

"Exactly," shouted Dave. "Now you've got it, Sally!"

"How can you use the three hows in other situations?" asked Sally.

"Let's say a customer walks into a jewelry store to buy a gift for his wife. The salesperson already starts to learn the *how will it be used* by the customer's opening statement. The next thing the salesperson does is ask him *how much* he is planning to spend. This keeps the salesperson from wasting both of their time by displaying something he isn't able or willing to afford. You know, Sally, I've been told by someone who used to work in a jewelry store that she was instructed to start by showing something more than what the customer asked for because chances are he or she would still spend it. This is bad sales and it's bad ethos. It blows up the member compass we talked about on Monday because the customer thinks the salesperson isn't listening and understanding. If the man says his limit is $300 and the salesperson starts by showing him a necklace for $600, he may think everything in the store is out of his price range, and he may walk out the door. A better option would be for the salesperson to start out by showing him something in his price range and then offer an alternative for something a little more."

"Determine *how soon* by asking the customer 'when do you need it?' If the customer has some time to make the purchase, maybe there is a sale coming up which will save him money. This may reduce the salesperson's commission, but the customer will be grateful and it will help build a relationship which could lead to more sales in the future. In this situation, if the gift is for Valentine's Day and he is walking in on February 13th, the how soon is pretty obvious."

"I never thought about that," said Sally. "Can you give me an example of when asking *how will* it be used helps to determine what product to offer?"

"Sure," Replied Dave. "Suppose a customer walks into a store to purchase a computer. If I am the salesperson, asking *'how will you use it?'* can determine if I should focus on a desktop or laptop. From there I can narrow down based on processor speed, memory, software, and other options. Maybe the customer would be better off with a tablet instead of a computer. When you find out how he or she plans to use it, you help uncover the third type of need, the unknown need."

"An unknown need, what's that?" asked Sally.

"An **unknown need** is when you discover a situation the customer was unaware of," replied Dave. "Let's say while you were talking to the customer about how he uses his computer, he mentions that he stores and edits a lot of photos he takes with his smartphone. When you ask him if

Uncovering the Need

he prints the photos himself, he says no, he prints them at the local drug store because the pictures look fuzzy when he prints them at home. You just discovered an unknown need for the customer—a new printer."

"That sounds like the type of sales I was afraid of," protested Sally. "It sounds like you're forcing something on them. Wouldn't customers know what they need when they come in?"

"Not really," replied Dave. "This brings up my fifth rule of sales:

Customers Often Don't Know What They Need.

"On Monday we discussed the customer compass and the customer's needs. Sometimes, they don't realize what those needs are. The customer looking to buy the computer doesn't know he also needs a new printer because his current printer works just fine based on the way he has always used it. After discovering he could save money if he printed photos at home instead of in the store, getting a new printer is now a need. In sales, not only do we call that an unknown need, we also refer to that as identifying the gap."

"Identifying the gap?" asked Sally sheepishly. "What is the gap?"

"The gap is the difference between the features and benefits of the customer's current product compared to the

- 55 -

customer's needs and wants. In this instance, the customer wants to print professional-looking photos but his printer isn't capable of doing so. That feature is the gap. Think about how many customers come in here with a gap in their banking relationship they may not even be aware of. On the wall is a poster advertising a very cheap auto loan rate. I bet a lot of people looking to buy a car ask you about that."

"Yes, we do," replied Sally. "It is a really good rate, much better than what other banks and local car dealers offer."

"That's great; is it just available for new purchases, or is it available for refinancing as well?" asked Dave.

"It's available for a refinance," replied Sally. "But we don't get too many people asking about that. It's usually just customers looking to purchase."

"That's what I thought," replied Dave. "This is what finding the gap and unknown needs are all about. Customers need a car loan to buy a car. After they get the loan, they tend to forget about it—except to make the monthly payments, that is. Customers know their monthly payment amount, but most don't know the rate of the loan. They may walk right by the poster for your car rate, but pay it no mind because they don't think they need a loan since they already have one. By talking with your customers you can uncover needs they didn't even know they had. This brings us back to your first customer of the day: Mrs. Little..."

Sally's Notebook

☑ Customers have immediate, future, and unknown needs.

☑ Ask the three how questions to determine the best product: how much, how soon, and how will you use it.

☑ Customers often don't know what they need.

☑ Identify the gap.

CHAPTER SIX

UNDERSTANDING THE *WHY* AND *BIG-PICTURE* QUESTIONS

Mr. and Mrs. Little are both in their late 50s. They are long-time customers and very friendly with Sally. The Littles have three children, the youngest of which recently moved out into an apartment of her own. Feeling their house was too big for just the two of them, the Littles recently moved into a smaller home in an over-55 community. As Sally provided this brief overview of the Little's situation, Dave listened intently.

"There could be plenty of unknown needs for the Littles" explained Dave. "You won't know until you start to uncover them with a conversation. If they moved into a smaller house, they probably lowered their expenses. Maybe they received money from the sale of their old house. They could be in a position where they have extra money for the first time in a long time and need someone to talk with about how to invest."

"You're right," replied Sally. "Mrs. Little told me last week that after the move they would be saving a lot of money. She said Mr. Little was planning on being able to retire in six or seven years. I guess they should talk to our investment consultant and see how he can help prepare them for retirement. I would never think a routine transaction such as a change of address could lead to a sales opportunity. I knew Mr. and Mrs. Little's situation, but how could I determine unknown needs from other people who do simple transactions, Dave? The transaction by itself doesn't provide any clues."

"That's true," said Dave. "Many times a transaction by itself doesn't tell you what the customer needs and wants. That's because the transaction by itself is not the reason for the sale, it is *why* the customer is performing the transaction. This leads me to my sixth rule of sales:

UNDERSTANDING WHY
WILL UNCOVER UNKNOWN NEEDS

"Mrs. Little changed her address because she recently moved. The reason why someone moves is usually a life-changing event such as a marriage, divorce, new job, bigger family, and so on. Those life-changing events come with needs and wants, which lead to sales opportunities. Many times customers are so involved with their event, they don't fully realize the needs and wants. They are so focused on what is happening right in front of them that they can't see the big picture. That's why a great salesperson needs to ask big-picture questions."

"That makes sense, Dave." said Sally. "Can you give me an example?"

"Sure. Let's say you just purchased your first home and you know you need a toaster. You walk into an appliance store and tell the salesperson what you're looking for. He gives you the option of a two-, four-, or six-slice toaster, each in different colors. Maybe he even discusses the benefits of a toaster oven over a traditional toaster. But if that is all you talk about, when you get home all you are going to be able to do is make toast! The salesperson should ask other questions, such as:

What other products do you have in your new home?

What type of products did you use in your old home?

What type of cooking do you expect to do?

"The answers to these big-picture questions will help uncover what other products you will need in your new home. Big-picture questions will help unlock a customer's unknown needs which lead to sales opportunities. This is true regardless of the type of business you're in. But you can only find the answer if you know the key"

"What's that?" asked Sally.

"You need to know how to listen," replied Dave. "Customers will almost always tell you their needs and wants, but they often do it indirectly. You need to listen to the things they say, and sometimes the things they don't, to uncover their needs—especially their unknown needs. Unfortunately, salespeople sometimes talk too much and end up talking themselves out of a sale. They are too preoccupied with presenting a product before truly understanding their customer's compass. Sally, have you ever read *The 7 Habits of Highly Effective People*, by Dr. Stephen Covey?"

"Yes, I have," replied Sally, "a couple of times. It's a very profound book."

"Yes, it is," said Dave. "In the book, Dr. Covey teaches us we should 'seek first to understand, then to be understood.' I think every sales person should learn and live that rule. Salespeople must practice their listening skills. Possession of good listening skills is an extremely important way to satisfy your customers' needs and wants. There are lots of good books and exercises to help you improve your listening skills. Here are a few tips to remember:

- Listening means silence. It is impossible to listen and talk at the same time.

- Respect pauses. Your customer may need to momentarily pause to collect their thoughts. Give them time to complete their thoughts before you respond.

- Don't assist the customer by finishing their thoughts for them. It's frustrating and embarrassing if you should finish their thoughts incorrectly.

- Acknowledge you are listening by periodically responding (nodding, "yes," "I understand").

- Ask for clarification if the customer's message is unclear. This will insure that you get the correct information.

- Recap main points during periodic breaks in the conversation.

- Take notes to concentrate on the main points, and to better determine your customer's needs and wants. This will provide you a reference point during and after the conversation.

"Listening really is a skill," said Sally. "I've been to seminars where the instructor had us practice listening exercises. It really does work. Dave, from what we have discussed so far, it seems that listening to the customer is the key to sales. Most of what you have taught me revolves around listening to the customer and understanding what is important to them."

"That is exactly right, Sally. Unless you know what's important to the customer, you have nothing to sell! Now that we have learned how to uncover the customer's needs and wants, tomorrow we will learn how to match the products and services to meet those needs."

As Dave finished his final thought, another employee approached Sally to interrupt the conversation. Mr. Kelly, a long-time customer, was in the branch asking to speak with Sally about changing the due date on a loan. Sally knew him well. She excused herself from Dave and walked over to where Mr. Kelly sat.

"Hi, Mr. Kelly. I haven't seen you in here in a while. I heard you are interested in changing the due date of your loan?"

"Yes," replied Mr. Kelly. "I need to reorganize my bills. I don't know if you heard, but the factory just had another round of layoffs, and unfortunately I was one of the ones called into the foreman's office. It's tough, Sally I was there for almost 30 years. I know I'll find a new job, but in the meantime all we have is unemployment benefits along with the income from Mrs. Kelly's part-time job."

"I'm really sorry to hear that, Mr. Kelly," responded Sally. "I had heard the factory was struggling, but I thought the future was starting to look a little brighter. Back in the day it was one of the largest companies in town."

"It sure was," said Mr. Kelly. "My brother worked there and so did many of our friends. When times were better, it was a great place. It was a union shop, and offered good pay and strong benefits."

Sally practiced her listening skills just as she and Dave had discussed. Suddenly a thought occurred to her. "Did the factory offer a pension?" she asked.

"Yes, it did."

"Can I ask what you plan to do with it?"

"I don't know, Sally. It's all very confusing," said Mr. Kelly. "The woman in HR gave me some paperwork about it and a number to call. One of the other guys told me we can just leave it in there until we retire. I've got at least another 15 years until I can start thinking about that. Of course, the money's just going to sit there. I have an option to take it with me, but I don't know the first thing about how to invest it. Besides, I heard I would have to pay taxes and penalties if I didn't put it in the right kind of account. Like I said, Sally, It's all so confusing; I thought it might be best to just leave it alone."

Sally listed to Mr. Kelly's concerns and was empathetic in her response. "I can really appreciate what a stressful time this is for you, Mr. Kelly. Many people feel the same way as you do: concerned about doing the wrong thing with their pension. Fortunately, we have an investment consultant, Pat Flannery, who specializes in helping customers invest for retirement. I've had him help a lot of my customers who are in situations similar to yours. He's even helped me invest my 401K account. I think it would be well worth sitting down and talking with him. I can give him your number to set up an appointment for you if that's OK."

"Thanks, Sally, that would be great," said Mr. Kelly appreciatively. "I didn't realize the bank offered services like that. I'm really appreciative of you looking out for me. This is why I keep banking here and like dealing with you," he smiled.

Sally completed the paperwork to change the due date for Mr. Kelly's loan. Afterwards she took down his information and reminded him that he would get a call from the investment consultant within a day or two. Mr. Kelly thanked her again, shook hands, and left. As he walked out the door, Dave congratulated Sally on a job well done.

"Fantastic job, Sally! That was a great example of uncovering an unknown need. Don't look now, but you're starting to sell!"

Sally knew it, and felt good about it. Her only regret now is she wished she had done it sooner.

Sally's Notebook

☑ Understanding "why" will uncover unknown needs.

☑ Ask the big-picture questions.

☑ Learn to listen to what the customer is really telling you.

CHAPTER SEVEN

WIIFM: SELLING THE BENEFITS

Thursday morning was the coldest it had been in weeks, and Dave was waiting at the branch for Sally when she arrived. "Good morning, Sally. I know it's going to be a long day today. I thought you might need something to help warm you up and keep you alert, so I brought you a hot coffee. I wasn't sure how you liked it, so I brought cream, sugar, and other sweeteners for you." Sally was much appreciative of Dave's gesture. Unbeknownst to her, Dave's greeting was also the beginning of today's lesson.

"We've talked about some of the mistakes salespeople make" announced Dave. "Here's another biggie—salespeople may actually lose a sale by selling the product or service."

Sally was confused. After all, she thought you were supposed to sell the product.

"The fact of the matter," said Dave, "is we sometimes try to sell things customers don't want. Think about it; how many people actually want a checking account? That's not really what we would call a sexy product, is it? Nobody's going to go to their bank, get a checking account, and go home to show it off to all of their friends. They don't go 'hey, come take a look at my new checking account I just got at the bank!' It's not the same thing as bringing home a big-screen television, or the latest-and-greatest smartphone or tablet."

"Customers don't necessarily want our products... they do want and need the things our products do for them. Consider our products and services to be the bridge our customers cross to meet up with their needs and wants. Customers don't necessarily want a checking account, but they need a way to pay their monthly bills. You won't have a customer come in here who wants to give you $350 a month for the next 5 years, but the same customer may want a new car so much that he or she *needs* a car loan and is willing to sacrifice those monthly payments."

"This is where the customer compass comes into play" acknowledged Sally, "distinguishing the customer's needs, wants, and sacrifices. Does this apply to other industries besides banking?"

"It sure does, Sally. I always tell people that nobody wants an exterminator; they just want to get rid of the bugs in their house and keep them from coming back. I don't particularly want a life insurance policy, but I want to know my wife and children are protected if anything ever happens to me. Depending on their industry, salespeople need to know that products and services don't necessarily sell themselves. We need to address our customer's WIIFM."

"I've heard that before," said Sally. "WIIFM—What's In It For Me?"

"Exactly," said Dave. "Customers want to know how purchasing a product or service is going to benefit them. That's the WIIFM. If there is nothing in it for the customer, then what's the point of them buying what you're trying to sell? We've talked over the last few days about uncovering the customer's needs, but sometimes the customer doesn't understand how the product really does fit his or her needs. All products have features and benefits. As a salesperson, it's important to both understand what they are and how to differentiate them from one another.

A **feature** describes a specific characteristic of a product. It does not change, regardless of who is looking or interacting with the product. For example, features of ice cream are that it is cold and sweet.

A **benefit** describes what the favorable outcome would be from using each particular feature. It addresses the WIIFM principle. I also like to say it answers the question 'so what?' The benefits of cold and sweet ice cream are that it cools you down on a hot summer day, and it tastes good.

"The product's features remain the same no matter who is looking at it. However, its benefits change all the time depending on the situation and the customer. The fact that ice cream cools you down is a benefit in the summer, but not so much in the winter. People up here in the north still eat ice cream in the winter, just not for the benefit of getting cooled down. I eat it in the winter because it's sweet and it tastes good. Now someone who may be diabetic won't see the benefit of eating ice cream made with sugar no matter what time of year it is. You see, Sally, benefits change all the time, and benefits are what drives customers to buy."

"Let me tell you a story about a man at a convention who was trying to sell a brand new product nobody had ever seen before. People walked by and picked the product up to look at it. The man carefully detailed all of the product's features and how it worked. People were overwhelmed by all the information. Some scratched their heads, and all put the item down and walked away. It was a few hours into the convention, and no one had bought the product. Suddenly, the man had an idea. A few minutes later another person came up to his table and picked up the item. Instead of describing it the man now said what it could do. He told the individual all of the convenient things this product would do for him and how it would make his life easier. The conventioneer was excited at the prospect and ending up buying it. There was a crowd beginning to form at the man's table. He continued selling the benefits to everyone who came up to look at the product. By the end of the day, he had sold every last one."

"Wow," responded Sally, "you can really see how selling the benefit makes a difference as opposed to trying to sell the features. It makes sense to me because I do make purchases based on what a product is going to do for me. I buy a specific type of laundry detergent because I like the way my clothes look and smell after I wash with it. I buy certain types of foods based on how tasty and healthy they are for my family and me. I'm already familiar with using these products. For new products, someone needs to tell me or show me the benefits to get me to buy."

"You got it exactly," exclaimed Dave. "This is a good time to bring up my seventh rule of sales:

BENEFITS SELL

"Each product has its own unique sets of benefits. The benefits may differ depending on the industry. Banking is pretty simple; our products deal with making or saving money, convenience, security, and peace of mind. A swimming pool store sells fun and relaxation. A jewelry store sells prestige and glamour."

"So far, we've talked a lot about uncovering the first two points of the customer's compass: needs and wants. Now it's time to talk about the third point—sacrifices. Customers know they can't enjoy all the benefits. While many benefits complement one another, others may conflict with each other. Sometimes customers have to sacrifice one benefit in order to obtain another. Let's say a customer in her 30s needs to make money for retirement. She may be willing to invest in high-risk stocks for the potential of a big return. In this case, she is sacrificing security for the greater benefit of making money. Now as that same person gets closer to retirement age, her priorities may shift. She may be more concerned with security and want to invest in something safer like a certificate of deposit. This leads me to my eighth rule of sales:

UNDERSTAND WHAT CUSTOMERS CARE ABOUT MOST

"Each customer is different; they have different needs, wants, and items they are willing to sacrifice. Not only do their needs differ from each other, a customer's need may change from one day to the next. During your conversation, you are uncovering what he or she cares about most at that point in time."

"Sally, does your family like pizza?"

"Of course. I thought everyone did."

"When you order, do you typically pick it up yourself or have it delivered?"

"It depends," replied Sally. "Most of the time my husband or I will pick it up on the way home from work, but sometimes we get it delivered."

Dave agreed that he and his wife were the same way. "We order from a place just a few minutes from our house. We tend to pick it up ourselves because we can get it sooner and save on the tip and delivery charge. In those instances, saving time and saving money are the benefits we care about most. But sometimes we don't feel like going out. Maybe there's something on TV we're both watching, or maybe it's really rainy outside. In those instances, we'll have it delivered. We know it will cost more, but the convenience of not having to leave the house is the benefit we care most about at that time.

"People are willing to sacrifice saving money in certain situations where another benefit is more appealing. Some people are willing to pay for convenience, even if it's not all the time, just like in our example with having pizza delivered. Some people will also pay for a nicer meal, especially if it's a special occasion"

"Sally, remember when I told you the story about the insurance agent trying to get me to switch my homeowner's insurance?"

Sally did remember the story. It coincided with Dave's third rule; *focus on what's important to the customer, not what's important to you.* The agent continuously focused on how Dave could save money by switching his homeowners insurance. Since Dave had a good experience with his company while neighbors had had bad experiences with theirs, he was more interested in maintaining his peace of mind by remaining with that agency rather than switching to the other one.

"The agent on the phone didn't try to understand that the benefit I cared about most in that situation was peace of mind," reminded Dave. "She assumed the only thing I would be interested in is saving money. If you don't uncover the right benefit, you are not going to get the sale. Sally, do you know one of the biggest fears that keeps people from trying to sell to customers?"

"Fear of rejection," responded Sally.

"Exactly!" exclaimed Dave. "The more rejection people receive, the less likely they are to continue to sell. I know hearing 'no' is part of the sales process; we are going to talk more about that tomorrow. I've heard managers use the old saying 'every *no* gets you closer to a *yes*.' I've heard managers tell struggling salespeople that they just needed to ask more people for a sale. Sally, that's hogwash! If an employee doesn't know how to discover what customers care about most, and how to sell the benefits, asking more people for the sale will simply result in more *no's*!

"When I talk about selling the benefits, you want to lead with the benefit before the product. Sally, tell me which of the following two statements sound more enticing to you:

If you refinance your car, you can save $1,000.

You can save $1,000 by refinancing your car.

"The second one sounded better to me," said Sally. "But aren't they really saying the same thing?"

"For the most part, they are," agreed Dave. "The first statement leads with the product: a car loan. But the second statement, the one that you liked better, leads with the benefit: save money. Most people relate better to the second statement. People tend to have a short attention span, and you only have a few seconds to keep their attention. Leading with a benefit statement, especially when you hit on what the customer cares about most, keeps their attention. I need a customer's attention to make a sale."

Sally really liked what Dave was saying. When she first heard Mr. Fox talk about the new sales culture at the big company-wide meeting, she envisioned her manager pushing to sell, sell, SELL! to each and every customer who walked through the door. She thought back to the day before and the unknown needs of both Mr. Kelly and Mrs. Little, and how selling really was service. She was now a firm believer in everything that Dave had said from the first day they met. Sally could become a great salesperson. She really enjoyed her meetings with Dave. Unfortunately, they would come to an end tomorrow.

Sally's Notebook

☑ Customers don't necessarily want the product, they want what the product can do for them.

☑ Benefits sell.

☑ Customers want to know "What's In It For Them."

☑ Understand what the customer cares about most.

CHAPTER EIGHT

CLOSING THE SALE

Friday morning. Sally had learned so much over the past four days with Dave, and today was their last day together. After each day's session she had used the skills learned to uncover customers' needs—needs which were there all along.

Dave arrived at the branch shortly after 10:00. He was eager to get started. "Sally, today is our last day together, and it's an important one. Now that we have learned how to determine customers' needs and wants, understand what he or she cares about most, match the best product or service, and present it by leading with the benefit, the only thing left to do is to close the sale. This is perhaps the most difficult step for people who are uncomfortable with selling. Not only is there a risk of rejection, like we discussed yesterday, but employees feel they are being pushy."

"Sally, let's say you went to training to learn CPR and how to administer the Heimlich Maneuver. Your training included how to recognize when a person is chocking and needs assistance. If you went out to a restaurant for dinner and you saw someone was in trouble and needed help, would you help him or would you be afraid you were being too pushy?"

"Of course I would help him," was Sally's reply.

"I would hope so" said Dave. "You immediately identified a need and provided a solution. The same holds true for my sales process. Needs-based selling is not being pushy. It's helping the customer reach their needs and wants. If I could save a customer $1,000 by refinancing his car loan with us, why wouldn't I want to close the sale? If I don't I'm actually making him pay $1,000 more than he should! That's not only poor selling, it's also bad service."

"Closing the sale starts with the very first word that you speak, and the very first action you take. Closing the sale is as important as opening it. Your customer needs to feel they have more than enough information to consider what you are offering them. Most people just simply need your encouragement. If you have followed all of the steps we talked about this week, asking for the sale will be a natural end to your conversation. Not only are you selling a product, but you are providing quality customer service."

"Employees who still feel nervous when asking for the sale may want to consider using a trial close. This will alleviate some of the pressure by checking for acceptance. After every few benefit statements, check with the customer by asking a trial close question, such as:

- How does all of this sound to you?

- I think it makes sense for your situation. What do you think?

- This sounds right for you; do you agree?

"With a trial close, you are not yet asking for the business. You are validating that you have really uncovered the solution to their needs and wants."

"A more direct way to close the sale is with an assumed close. The assumed close guides customers into saying yes. You are telling them that, based on your experience, the products and services you recommend are the perfect fit to satisfy their needs and wants. An assumed close sounds something like this:

- I think this product makes a lot of sense for you. Let's go ahead and open up this account.

- It sounds like this is going to satisfy all of your banking needs. Let's go ahead and open it up for you today.

"This sounds great," said Sally, "but I always had a problem with handling objections. What happens when I perform all the steps correctly and the customer still objects to the sale?"

"Nobody likes to hear 'no' from the customer," said Dave. "We said yesterday how fear of rejection was one of the reasons people tend to not ask for the sale. Following these steps should reduce the number of times a customer tells you no, though it will still happen. While we don't like to hear an objection, it tells us that a customer does not see the benefit of a product, or that we didn't really uncover what the customer cares about most. It may also uncover a hidden concern that is preventing him or her from completing the sale."

"There are a few steps you should take to manage and, hopefully, overcome your customer's objection or concern.

- Stay calm and professional. LISTEN to what the customer is saying and not saying. Maybe you have misread what is important to the customer.

- Paraphrase the objection: *If I understand correctly, you are unsure about _____. Is that correct?*

- If you are not sure of the objection, ask an open-ended question to find out more.

- Use the **feel-felt-found** technique: *I appreciate the way you feel, many of my customers have **felt** the same way, and they have **found** that switching accounts worked out for the best.* While customers don't want to be the last person on the block to try something, they don't necessarily want to be the first either. The feel-felt-found technique lets them know others have been in the same situation and it has worked out well for them.

- Respond with additional benefit statements.

"After you feel you have addressed the objection, it's a good idea to obtain acceptance again from the customer. Ask a trial question to determine if you have overcome the member's objection."

"OK, but what about a customer who says he or she needs to go home and think about it?" asked Sally. "I get a lot of customers who tell me that. Or they'll say they need to talk it over with their husband or wife."

"That's normal, especially if you've uncovered a future or an unknown need. Remember, by definition, a future need means the customer isn't ready to buy now. He or she is gathering information to act later. You need to respect that and allow the customer to leave without making the sale. Trying to put on the pressure won't increase your chances of making the sale right now, and it may prevent you from making the sale in the future."

"In these instances it's important to set a time to follow up with the customer at their convenience, and make sure to follow up. Let's say a customer comes in at the beginning of the year to inquire about a loan for a home project, but wants to wait until the spring to get started. You should provide the information and then agree on a time, and note when to call the customer to follow up. Sometimes I see employees make the mistake of simply offering their business card to customers and assume they will make the call. This leads me to my ninth rule of sales:

OVERALL, CUSTOMERS PROCRASTINATE AND ARE REACTIVE

"There is no guarantee the customer will call back. If you want the sale, you should be the one who takes the proactive approach to call the customer. I have a friend who called a few insurance companies to get some life insurance quotes. He was in no big rush to get the policy, and wanted to compare rates. He called about a dozen companies in all, gave them all of his information, and told them he would get back to them. Two weeks passed when one of the companies called him back asking if he had any additional questions about the information provided, and if not if he was ready to proceed. My friend went ahead and got a policy with that company. They didn't offer the cheapest rate, but they were the one to take the initiative and call him back."

"When you uncovered an unknown need, customers may also need time to think about and digest the situation. You want to schedule a time to follow up with them as well, preferably within a week. If the customer tells you he needs to go home to talk it over with his wife, ask for a follow-up time when both will be home so you can answer any questions she might have as well."

"Dave, thank you so much for all of your help" said Sally appreciatively. "I must admit a lot of employees were nervous when we heard about this new sales-centric environment, and I was one of them. I was also very skeptical when I heard I would be meeting with a sales coach. You've shattered all of the perceptions I had about sales. I always had a negative opinion of sales. I thought sales was pushing products that people didn't need, want, or could afford. Your first rule of sales was sales is service, and you have demonstrated that ever since. I've come to realize that I've been selling my entire career, I just never got around to actually asking for the sale. By not asking for the sale, I was doing a disservice to my customers."

"Sally, I really enjoyed our time together" replied Dave. "As I told you all along, I really believe you will end up being the top salesperson here at Friendly Community Bank. You care about your customers and believe in your products and services. I knew you were going to be great at sales from the moment I heard about you because of the way you treat your customers, which brings me to my tenth and final rule of sales:

SELLING IS EASY WHEN YOU DON'T CONSIDER IT SELLING.

Sally couldn't agree more.

Sally's Notebook

☑ Closing the sale begins with the first words you say.

☑ Objections mean the customer doesn't see the benefits of using the product.

☑ Customers procrastinate and are reactive.

☑ Selling is easy when you don't consider it selling.

CHAPTER NINE

EPILOGUE

It has been just over three years since Mr. Fox became the new CEO at Friendly Community Bank. During this time Sally became one of the top sales performers in the company, just as Dave predicted. Sally had a knack for talking with customers and finding opportunities to save them money by refinancing loans or switching over their accounts. Sally had more repeat business from customers by far, and they frequently referred friends and family to meet with her as well. Sally consistently exceeded her monthly goals and was named salesperson of the year for two consecutive years.

Sally vividly remembered that day at the company-wide meeting when Mr. Fox announced the new sales culture. She had doubted that she would spend three more weeks at the bank, let alone three more years. She was sure she was going to hate it. But to be truthful, it was some of the most enjoyable time she spent there. Never before did she have a greater sense of importance, working closely with her customers to help them meet their banking needs and wants.

Although Sally enjoyed her success, she knew the end was approaching. She had talked about it with her husband for a few months and finally made her decision. One Monday morning she walked into her manager's office and handed her a typed letter in an envelope. Sally was retiring.

After thirty-five years in banking, the last twenty-three at Friendly Community Bank, Sally's banking career was coming to an end in just under a month. Sally gave her boss twice the standard two-week notice because she felt they deserved the consideration. She also wanted the opportunity to say good-bye to the many customers who made up her extended family. She even received a card in the mail from Dave, with a note written on the inside cover:

Sally,

Congratulations on your retirement. It was such a pleasure to get to know you and work with you years ago. I knew when we first met you would be a natural

at sales. I am so proud of you and all of your accom-
plishments. Good luck in whatever you decide to do
next.

Your Sales Coach,
Dave Kimba

Sally was really glad to hear from Dave. He made such an impact on the end of her career. If it wasn't for his guidance, she would have probably retired three years earlier. She would have missed out on the relationships she built and strengthened, and the people she helped achieve their needs and wants through the sales process Dave taught her.

On her next-to-last day at the bank, Sally had a meeting with Miss Kyleigh Raymond from Human Resources to conduct her exit interview. She talked for nearly an hour about how much she enjoyed working there and the wonderful opportunities the bank afforded her. As the meeting neared a close, Miss Kyleigh Raymond had one question for Sally: "what could we do to get you to stay?"

Sally was honored by her question, although she was sure it was asked only out of politeness. "I've worked ever since I graduated from high school. It's time to take a break. My manager offered me a part-time position, but even that is too much of a commitment right now. I would probably be able to work here and there from time to time, but nobody has a position like that."

Miss Raymond smiled at Sally and thanked her for her service. "Before you leave, Mr. Fox asked if you could stop by for a minute. I'll walk you over."

"What a nice gesture," thought Sally. She had never met Mr. Fox one-on-one before. He had visited her branch a few times over the years, and presented her with her Salesperson of the Year award, but they never had a full conversation. As they came to Mr. Fox's office, Miss Raymond told the secretary Sally was here to see him. The secretary told them they were expected and could go right in.

When Sally walked through the door, Mr. Fox greeted her immediately. "Hello, Sally. Thank you for stopping by. Please have a seat. I want to personally thank you for your years of service at Friendly Community Bank." Mr. Fox and Sally continued with some small talk which included her plans for retirement. After a minute or two, Mr. Fox had a question.

"Sally, as happy as I am for your retirement, it pains me to see such a great salesperson leave the organization completely. Miss Raymond from HR texted me as you two were wrapping up your meeting that you would be interested in working from time to time. Is that something you would consider if we had a position like that available?" Sally was flattered. "Yes, Mr. Fox. That is something I would seriously consider doing. Do you have something like that available in the branch?"

"Actually, I do. It's not exactly the same position as you have now, but I know you'll be great. You would probably work only five or six weeks out of the year, every couple of months. It does involve a little bit of travel, which we would pay for. It's a great position Sally, and I'd really like to offer it to you now."

"What is it?" asked Sally.

"A sales coach."

Dave Kimba's
10 Rules of Sales

1. Sales is Service.

2. You can't sell what you don't know.

3. Focus on what's important to the customer, not what's important to you.

4. Be someone the customer likes and trusts.

5. Customers often don't know what they need.

6. Understanding why will uncover unknown needs.

7. Benefits sell.

8. Understand what customers care about most.

9. Overall, customers procrastinate and are reactive.

10. Selling is easy when you don't consider it selling.

ABOUT THE AUTHOR

Michael Patterson is a speaker, trainer, and author who has been developing managers and employees to reach their fullest potential since 2000. Specializing in leadership, employee development, and sales topics, he relies on 25 years of banking and retail experience to incorporate personal stories into his presentations. Michael is currently responsible for the training and development of a $1.5 billion, 300-employee credit union in southeastern Pennsylvania.

Michael lives in suburban Philadelphia with his wife Ann, their daughter Kyleigh, and two dogs, Bailey and Kimba. His dogs played a key role in his last book, *Sit Stay Succeed! Management Lessons from Man's Best Friend* (Tremendous Life Books: 2012).

Michael is a registered Pennsylvania Interscholastic Athletic Association (PIAA) sports official and former coach. Visit him at his website www.MikePat.com

NOTES

NOTES

NOTES

NOTES

NOTES

NOTES

NOTES

NOTES

NOTES

NOTES

NOTES

NOTES